RE-SOURCING

Laura Shamas

BROADWAY PLAY PUBLISHING INC
224 E 62nd St, NY, NY 10065
www.broadwayplaypub.com
info@broadwayplaypub.com

First printing: August 2008
I S B N: 0-88145-397-8

Book design: Marie Donovan
Word processing: Microsoft Word
Typographic controls: Ventura Publisher
Typeface: Palatino
Printed and bound in the U S A

CHARACTERS & SETTING

DAUBNEY, *male, Ameriblaze supervisor, thirty-five-ish*
JIMMIE ALICE, *female, Ameriblaze worker, late twenty-ish*
REECE, *male, Ameriblaze worker, African American,*
  thirty-forty-ish
MELBA, *female, Ameriblaze worker, forty-ish*
VIJAY, *male, Indian-American, thirty-forty-ish*
SELENA, *female, V P of Ameriblaze, thirty-forty-ish*

Ethnicities open for all characters except REECE *and* VIJAY.

Time: Right now

Place: Paris, Arkansas and Houston, Texas

*Settings: In a call center, in a bar, in a living room,
in a diner, on the street, in an office, in a restaurant, etc.
Area staging.*

Ninety minutes, no intermission.

RE-SOURCING was originally produced by John Halbert and Mapala Productions at the Noho Arts Center, Los Angeles, California, from 15 October to 21 November 2004. The cast and creative contributors were:

DAUBNEY . . . . Paul Kouri
JIMMIE ALICE . . . . Corrina Lyons
REECE . . . . K J Middlebrooks
MELBA . . . . Andi Matheny
VIJAY . . . . .Ravi Kapoor
SELENA . . . . Margot Foley

Understudies . . . . Subhash Mandal & Erwin Stone

Director . . . . Jules Aaron
Assistant director . . . . .Subhash Mandal
Production stage manager. . . . . .Andrea Covell

The play was developed further at Williamstown Theater Festival, July 2006 (Reading Series).

For my friend Jules Aaron,
whose direction of three of my plays
(including this one),
has meant the world to me

Scene One

(As the lights come up, four people sit at a phone bank linked to computer screens, near center stage, wearing headsets. They sit in this order: DAUBNEY, MELBA, REECE *and* JIMMIE ALICE. *The phones are incredibly active, and light up like crazy. Note: Some of the lines on pages 1-2 should be overlapped in this way: wherever the hyphen exists in the line above, ie, the next actor should start speaking his or her line.)*

DAUBNEY: Ameriblaze. America's hottest software provider. Can I help—you?

MELBA: Ameriblaze. America's hottest—software provider. Can I help you?

REECE: Ameriblaze—America's hottest software provider.

JIMMIE ALICE: Ameriblaze—

DAUBNEY: Ameriblaze software is compatible with Airport Extreme Base Station—

MELBA: Ameriblaze—

REECE: Ameriblaze—

JIMMIE ALICE: —Officially we aren't supposed to get into that, but off the record, it's your lucky day because I actually know how to fix that—problem.

MELBA: Click "Internet Connection". Now select T C P Script—

DAUBNEY: Ameriblaze—

REECE: You're going to need to reboot. Be sure to hold down the option key while—yeah, you're doing it.

JIMMIE ALICE: Ameriblaze—America's hottest software provider.

MELBA: No. That was T C P Script, not P C P Script. Keep scrolling—T as in Tom, not P as in Pie.

REECE: Ameriblaze—

DAUBNEY: Hit the return key. You're almost done.

DAUBNEY: Ameriblaze—

JIMMIE ALICE: Thanks for calling Ameriblaze—

REECE: Thanks for calling Ameriblaze—

MELBA: Thanks for calling Ameriblaze—

DAUBNEY: And thank you for calling Ameriblaze.

(Suddenly, it is quiet for ten to twenty seconds: The phones do not light up. Then, the four look at each other, as if to say, "What's wrong?" Each start to adjust their computer screens.)

DAUBNEY: Now what? The frickin' system's down?

REECE: My screen's dead.

JIMMIE ALICE: Mine, too.

MELBA: Ditto.

(DAUBNEY stands up and bangs on a screen. Then, strangely, from directly above, six pink envelopes fall, and land in front of each of them. One by one, with trepidation, they slowly take their headsets off, and open the pink envelopes. Together, they gasp, then scream. The other two unopened envelopes lie to the side.)

DAUBNEY, JIMMIE ALICE, REECE & MELBA: *Ahhhhhhh!*

(Then, they hold up the pink slips of paper that were in the envelopes, reading the fine print.)

DAUBNEY: Holy F-in' mackerel.

MELBA: Oh my god.

JIMMIE ALICE: Oh my god.

REECE: Am I readin' this right? *(Holds it close)*

DAUBNEY: They can't do this! They can't just frickin' do this.

MELBA: No notice. Thirty days of severance! I got two kids to support.

JIMMIE ALICE: Oh my god.

REECE: Oh, man. My chest is tight. *(He sits and takes deep breaths.)*

DAUBNEY: *(Throws headset down)* Damn it. It can't happen to us. It just can't.

MELBA: That V P Hodson didn't have the nerve to tell us herself. And she was just here.

REECE: And we all kissed her ass. *(He takes a few more deep breaths.)*

MELBA: The bitch...

DAUBNEY: *(Putting it together)* Yeah, she must have known. That's why she came all the way up here....

JIMMIE ALICE: Oh my god. *(To REECE)* You havin' an attack?

REECE: *(Shaking his head "no")* I got rent to pay.

DAUBNEY: We all got rent to pay, man. What'll I tell the wife—

MELBA: Shit. There's two extra slips here addressed to Sam and Juanita.

JIMMIE ALICE: This news'll ruin their vacations. They'll be comin' back to nothin'!

REECE: Whew-oo. *(Lets out a gasp of air)* This is it, then. *(Moves away from phone bank, picks up jacket from his chair.)* Time to walk away, folks. This is the big goodbye.

DAUBNEY: Can they do this? Can they just *do* this?

MELBA: *(Shaking her head)* They're doin' it, sugar cheeks. Big time. Can't believe it. Can't believe it. *(Grabs her purse, lights a cigarette.)*

JIMMIE ALICE: They *can* do it. They *are* doin' it. *(She starts to put on a coat on the back of her chair. She looks like she's going to cry.)*

DAUBNEY: Well, what are we gonna do 'bout it?

REECE: What do you mean, "do"? We can't do a thing. They're undoin' us, Daub.

DAUBNEY: Come on. I mean, are we men or what?

(MELBA gestures to JIMMIE ALICE and then back to herself.)

MELBA: *(Puffing on cig)* We're "or what," 'case you hadn't noticed.

DAUBNEY: I mean, are we meek human beings or are we fighters? Are we mice or are we Americans?

REECE: I'm not in the mood for twenty questions. I gotta go find a new job. I got a mother to support.

(REECE gathers up more of his belongings. JIMMIE ALICE stops.)

JIMMIE ALICE: I—I—I'm an American, Daubney. *(She bursts into tears.)*

MELBA: Who're you plannin' to fight, Mister Rabble Rouser? *(Comforts JIMMIE ALICE)* Honey, you're gonna be okay. You are....It's just a shock. This your first time? The first pink slip's always the worst.

DAUBNEY: Well, not that I believe in workin' with the gavel-thumpers and ambulance chasers. But surely there's a lawsuit here. I mean, the big shots at Ameriblasé can't just frickin' *outsource* us out of the blue like this, and get away with it. Were any of you

"not-i-fied" that we were "performin' poorly"?
They told me the opposite.

REECE: Yeah, you had a rocket in your pocket.
That's why they made you Supervisor and told
you everything.

DAUBNEY: I was on track to move up to V P.

REECE: And you're tellin' us for real that you weren't
in this loop? And that you didn't know the axe was
comin'?

DAUBNEY: No F-in' way.

REECE: Right. For all I know, you could be off to
Houston tomorrow for a big fat job at headquarters.

DAUBNEY: No. I'm not. I'll be back on the street lookin'
for a job, like y'all. And I'm real pissed off about it.

REECE: Yeah? I'd like to think you didn't sell us out.

DAUBNEY: I didn't. I swear.

(JIMMIE ALICE *wails again.*)

MELBA: Jimmie Alice. Honey. You okay?

JIMMIE ALICE: *(Dabbing eyes)* No. No, I'm not okay.
This job is my whole—was my whole life. Well, almost...
I do still have the book group.

DAUBNEY: Okay, okay. Listen, let's all go out for a drink
or something. We can't say goodbye like this.

REECE: A drink? Now? *(Looks at his watch)* It's two-thirty.

DAUBNEY: I'd say our shift is officially over. I'll buy.

REECE: *(Suspiciously)* You've never done that before.
Now that you're out of a job, you're gonna buy us all
a drink?

DAUBNEY: Okay, so I never got it together as Supervisor to help us socialize. At least I can make sure we wallow like hogs in misery together here at the end.

MELBA: *(Flirty)* Hell, I ain't had a drink with you since the Christmas party, Daub.

DAUBNEY: Well then? For old time's sake?

REECE: Okay. One drink. Just 'cause I'm worried about her. *(Indicates* JIMMIE ALICE*)*

*(*JIMMIE ALICE *wails again.* REECE *puts his arm around her, comforting her. Blackout)*

Scene Two

(Lights fade up on the four of them in a bar, stage left. They sit on stools. All are tipsy. A faintly raucous yet trendy country western bar song plays in the background. They sip drinks at various times throughout the scene.)

DAUBNEY: And that's how they did it on *Friends*. They all stuck together. They shoved it to N B C.

REECE: Man, you're missin' a big link. They were negotiatin' jobs that they still *had*. They were big T V stars.

JIMMIE ALICE: *(Slurs speech)* David Schwimmer was not a big star then. Not in '95.

REECE: But we're not negotiatin.' We're fired. The reason that so-called "elimination reality shows" are so popular is that in this economy, more and more Americans are gettin' sacked...

MELBA: I like the idea of stickin' together with you, Daub. I like it a lot. *(Quietly)* Are you and Karen still talkin' 'bout a separation?

(MELBA *winks at* DAUBNEY. *He moves his stool away from her slightly.*)

DAUBNEY: No comment. And maybe you should hold up on the 'ritas, Mel.

(DAUBNEY's *response irritates* MELBA, *and she scoots away from him.*)

JIMMIE ALICE: Where did our jobs go? They were outsourced, but to where? Texas? New Mexico? Mexico?

REECE: *(Shrugs)* Dunno. Don't care.

JIMMIE ALICE: Why don't we try to find 'em?

DAUBNEY: They went to India, of course. Prolly to Bangalore. Or New Del high.

REECE: Yeah, so now when they call for customer service, they'll get someone who says *(Imitates Indian accent)*: "Since when are you having this problem?"

DAUBNEY: Hey, not bad, dude.

REECE: They try to train 'em to sound American. Sometimes, they make the folks losin' the jobs train their replacements. We're lucky we didn't have to go through that.

DAUBNEY: Yeah, my replacement got real lucky 'cause right now, I'd like to kill him. Or her. Whoever or wherever they are.

JIMMIE ALICE: Reece, hey, I saw somethin' 'bout that on P B S. They take classes in American culture and all. They try to U S-ize 'em to sound more like us on the phone. They make 'em go watch a lot of American movies and sitcoms.

DAUBNEY: *(Snorting)* P B S! That's for liberal wackos.

MELBA: Once I called in an airline reservation to American Airlines, and the guy who took my order was in prison, in Oregon.

REECE: Always a comfort to give your credit card number to a convict, isn't it?

MELBA: They still outsource lots of cheap labor jobs to prisons...I think I'd rather my job'd gone to someone in prison. At least it would've kept it in the country.

JIMMIE ALICE: Except...that it gives a job to a convicted criminal...

DAUBNEY: But at least the criminal is a real American.

REECE: A telemarketer for A T & T called me the other day. I asked her where she was calling from, and she said *(Uses Indian accent)*: "Fairfax, Virginia." Riiiight. At least the corporations could let 'em all tell the truth. *(Takes a drink)*

JIMMIE ALICE: On the P B S special, it showed how they teach 'em down home chitchat. They learn the "American idiom". They explain slang, like "Stop yankin' my chain". And "Give me a ballpark figure".

DAUBNEY: What numbnuts. Like you can learn to speak American.

JIMMIE ALICE: They upload web sites with tons of info, like how hot it is that day in whatever town you're callin' from.

DAUBNEY: Wait. Wait! *(A quick beat)* That's it. You're brilliant, Reece and Jimmie A. *(He stands up and embraces* REECE.*)* Props to you, dude.

REECE: Whoa, hey guy. We're not that close or that wasted....

JIMMIE ALICE: What'd I say?

DAUBNEY: Y'all have just come up with our plan of attack.

REECE: What?

JIMMIE ALICE: What?

MELBA: What?

DAUBNEY: We're going to get our old jobs back.

REECE: How?

DAUBNEY: *(Standing up)* We are going stay right here and pretend to be Indian.

(A beat)

JIMMIE ALICE: Huh?

MELBA: I am part Indian. Check the official rolls. My grandfather was part Choctaw from Oklahoma.

REECE: Me, too. I got some Cherokee on my mom's—

DAUBNEY: No, no. Listen. We are going to pretend to be from *India*. The country, as in somewhere near Pakistan. We're gonna to band together and fool some big fat cat company—maybe ole Ameriblasé herself *(Holds up his pink slip)*—into hirin' us to work their phone centers.

REECE: *(Shaking head)* Daub, take two aspirins and call us in the morning.

DAUBNEY: Mister, I'm as churned up as a June twister, and I'm not going to sit and take this B S. I'm gonna protest! Think of what it'll do to this town to go through another shutdown. It'll be death. They closed the railways and the mines last century. Now they're tryin' to slam us again by closin' this call center? I'm gonna do the American thing and *stop them*. We can't let 'em get away with it. Let's *protest*!

JIMMIE ALICE: You? Protest?

REECE: Now how'll that possibly work? The head honchos at Ameriblasé *(Refers to pink slip)* know us. They sure as hell know you, the ex-Super. They know we're not in Bangalore.

DAUBNEY: See, here's the beauty of it. We'll...we'll... *(A pause, then divine inspiration)* hire someone who is

Indian-American to act as our front man! He goes to Houston and sweet-talks Hodson, tells her we're in Bangalore. They ain't gonna fly out to Bangalore to check on the facilities. Trust me. They're too cheap for that. They'll take us based on his pitch, and some dummied photos of a call center. Whatever. They'll never actually see us. This guy agrees to keep our secret, somehow, for some reason, I dunno why—prolly money—we'll work that out later. And then we won't need new jobs! We can stay here and keep our lives same as before as we *protest this outrageous act of corporate F-in' malfeasance*—

JIMMIE ALICE: New jobs don't exist any way, no matter what the administration says. They've all been outsourced and outmoded, and none are comin' back—

DAUBNEY: And *voilà*, we've pulled off the ultimate twenty-first century corporate revenge shaft plan.

MELBA: *(Applauds)* Woo-hoo! I like the sound of that. Those Ameribastards. They deserve it.

REECE: Wait, wait, wait. First of all, we'd have to take a pay cut in order to get our jobs back. That's the reason we got tossed. Workers in India'll do it for a third of our salaries. One third of our pay is big money there.

JIMMIE ALICE: That's fine. That's fine. I'll do triple overtime. I don't mind. This job's my life. Y'all are my life. Almost. Viva Les Proletariats!

MELBA: Hey. You know...We could forward some of the phone lines so they could be answered from our homes...The calls come in cycles. We could alternate late night shifts, if we had to, so no one person always has to handle all the late calls...

JIMMIE ALICE: Hey, we can run a fake call center from my house, since I live alone.

REECE: Whoa. Hey. Do the math, folks. Three times the work? Don't tell me you're actually considerin' this, Mel?

MELBA: Well, what do we have to lose? Towns all over the country are just closin' up due to this outsourcing biz. Places like Clintwood and Brownsville. I been readin' about it but I never thought it'd happen right here in Paris.

JIMMIE ALICE: Me neither.

MELBA: I don't wanna uproot. I love this town. My kids love it. All three of my exes live here. And this idea is...well, it's crazy all right. But it feels better than just gettin' canned and doin' nothin'. No one posts any Paris, Arkansas jobs on Craigslist, right? And bein' American means takin' crazy action, right?

JIMMIE ALICE: Two hundred and somethin' years ago, dumpin' Indian tea outta ships in Boston was crazy, too. Right? Right?

REECE: Okay, fine. Let's skip the logistics for a moment. How'll you possibly find someone who'll risk doing this, someone who'll pretend to represent us? Why would anyone in his right mind do that, and keep it a secret? It's stupid.

(A beat)

JIMMIE ALICE: *(Tipsy)* I don't know. We need a certain political operative type. I might have a way to find someone.

REECE: You?

DAUBNEY: How?

JIMMIE ALICE: Well, some nights, I hang out in the Arkansas Underground Chat Room online. Okay, every night. I post ads in there tryin' to get people for my political book group.

REECE: Oh. It's a *political* book group. I thought it was just a book group. I mighta wanted to join that. Shoulda told me.

JIMMIE ALICE: Yes, it's a political book group. My dream's to be featured on one of those liberal radio networks for startin' it. I never knew y'all well enough to go into it before. I thought I'd get fired if I discussed politics in the workplace. I mean, since the Patriot Act, I've been afraid to speak my mind anywhere except the 'net.... Actually, I've been kinda scared to *think*, too, in case the Attorney General and his fascist truth squad can mind-read. Anyway, I could post in the chat room asking specifically for an India-American expert. Someone really great might turn up. The 'net has a broad reach.

MELBA: Oh, what're the odds? We're in Paris.

DAUBNEY: It's cool. You might as well try. Someone might be willin' to drive in from Fort Smith.

REECE: *(Shaking head)* Y'all are too drunk to think straight. Thank God Sam and Juanita're gone for two weeks or he'd be hoarse by now and she'd be foamin' at the mouth from screamin'.

MELBA: Look. If anybody responds to the ad, I'm in. *(Raises her hand)*

JIMMIE ALICE *(Raises hand)* In.

DAUBNEY: *(Raises hand)* In.

REECE: Out.

DAUBNEY: Out? You and Jimmie frickin' thought of this.

REECE: No. *You* thought of it, Daub. You always try to pin your own bad ideas on others. Did they teach you that in management school? I said a few English words with a bad Indian accent. Jimmie A. talked about P B S. Then *you* thought of this jackass plan. But you credited it to us, tryin' to get us involved in a subconscious way, usin' psychological transference or whatever. This is a crazy, cockamamie idea, and tomorrow, when y'all're sober, you're gonna thank me for bein' the voice of reason in this pathetic situation. *Do not do this. Repeat. Do not do this.*

(A beat)

JIMMIE ALICE: Reece, does that mean you're really out or just sorta out?

REECE: Oh, Jimmie A, totally out. And y'all are totally out of it!

(Blackout)

Scene Three

(JIMMIE ALICE's living room. A spot on JIMMIE ALICE, stage right, as she types eagerly at her laptop computer screen. There are two empty beer bottles, and one half empty one on her table. She reads aloud what she types.)

JIMMIE ALICE: "Seeking India-American political expert for Paris, Arkansas underground political book group. Prefer.... *(She thinks, then types)* open-minded candidate with in-depth knowledge of twenty-first century India technological capabilities... *(Pauses, thinks, then types)* ...and a healthy dose of skepticism...and anger towards greedy, corporate insensitive American fat cats who sell out the little people while they rake in gazillions at our expense..." *(She sits back and takes a drink of beer. It feels good to have gotten that out. Suddenly, there's the magical chime sound of new mail: "You've Got Mail!").* Wow, that was fast! *(She rapidly types back.)* Why, hello, "Vijay Smith.... My name's Jimmie Alice...."

(The rapid typing of the keyboard is heard. Blackout)

Scene Four

(Lights up, stage right. A day later. VIJAY *sits in* JIMMIE ALICE'S *living room.* DAUBNEY *and* MELBA *are there, too.* JIMMIE ALICE *serves coffee to everyone. Note:* VIJAY *speaks with a New Jersey accent.)*

DAUBNEY: Okay, well, this is the group. What do you think?

VIJAY: *(Puts coffee down)* You seem like a very nice book club...different than I expected *(Quickly recovering)* ...I mean that in a good way.

JIMMIE ALICE: You seem very nice, too. I'm so glad you answered my drunk chat room post! You're perfect— for our group. And you've handled all of our questions about your background. Right, everybody?

*(*JIMMIE ALICE *looks to the others; they nod. It's kind of awkward, as none of the Arkansas trio knows what to do next.)*

MELBA: Yes, perfect. We love freelance programmers. And to think you've just moved here to Paris...

DAUBNEY: Yeah, now that I know you're from Jersey and love Springsteen, I'm comfortable. Welcome to our neck of the woods.

JIMMIE ALICE: Welcome.

MELBA: Welcome.

VIJAY: And you're all fast readers?

MELBA: Purty fast—

JIMMIE ALICE: Fast as a jack rabbit on ice. Why?

VIJAY: Because I really want to sink my teeth into some *(Quick beat)* ...thick underground subversive books which rail against big American fat cat corporations.

JIMMIE ALICE: Oh. So do we. Big time.

MELBA: And we will. Right, Jimmie Alice?

JIMMIE ALICE: Right. Absolutely.

VIJAY: You meet every month?

DAUBNEY: Correct.

VIJAY: Sooooo, what'd you read last month?

MELBA: Uh....

DAUBNEY: *(Nudges* JIMMIE ALICE*)* Jimmie A?

JIMMIE ALICE: *(Nervously)* Was it that Bible of all political book groups: *Lying Lying Liars and the Crazy Liars Who*...whatever the title is, you know, Al Franken's book? And before that, somethin' by...by the late Molly Ivins? And somewhere in there, we read something by someone who was a spy or whatever...

VIJAY: Okay. Seriously, now. Level with me. *(Pause)* You're not really a book group. You're...maybe into something more...explosive?

*(*JIMMIE ALICE, MELBA *and* DAUBNEY *exchange glances.)*

JIMMIE ALICE: Well, I do try to run a very small political book group. We're just very seriously in-between members.

(There's a pause.)

VIJAY: You can be straight with me.

*(*MELBA *and* JIMMIE ALICE *look at* DAUBNEY. *He shurgs, and them motions "okay".)*

MELBA: We aren't really part of her book group.

DAUBNEY: We're a fired crew of Paris call center workers whose jobs went to India. We're pissed and we want revenge.

JIMMIE ALICE: *(Pumps fist)* Yeah! We want to take back America.

MELBA: What we want is—we want to find someone who'll pretend to be our boss at a fake call center, which we're gonna pretend is in Bangalore, India.

DAUBNEY: See, we're going to pretend to be Indian workers. We just need someone who can pretend to be our boss, and sell it to Houston.

JIMMIE ALICE: And that way, we'll get our old jobs back, and earn a third of what we used to. And make a political statement all at the same time. Isn't it brilliant?

DAUBNEY: It's our twenty-first century corporate revenge shaft plan!

(There's a pause.)

VIJAY: *(Bemused)* This is a goof, right?

DAUBNEY: No. No. We want you to be our front man. We want to pay you for a one-time participation, to act like you're our boss from Bangalore, and pitch us to our old company. And then, of course, never tell anyone. Ever...I guess sign a contract or somethin' to that effect.

VIJAY: *(Scratches his head)* You're not putting me on?

JIMMIE ALICE: We're serious. I swear. What do ya think?

(A beat)

VIJAY: Uh, uh, I don't know what to say. I mean, it is interesting from both a geo-political and a naïve, neo-political perspective. And legally, one could argue that it is a bonafide act of political protest—in the event that you got caught.

JIMMIE ALICE: What could they catch us for? Voluntarily workin' for cheap salaries and no benefits? We'd be the poster children for the administration's Department of Labor. Look at the record on minimum wage and overtime. And how would we ever get caught? It took them five years to nail the Enron guys. We're small potatoes and few to a hill.

MELBA: Yes, but the government loves to scapegoat the little people.

JIMMIE ALICE: Basically, if you're not white, male, rich or famous, you're screwed in the American judicial system-but I don't think they'd catch us. We're so under the radar—

MELBA: *(Aside to* DAUBNEY*)* I never knew Jimmie was such a radical politico. Did you?

DAUBNEY: Noooooo.

VIJAY: *(Wheels in motion)* Okay, okay...I do think you could characterize this as a legal, political act of protest. You'd be doing the actual work. What I like about it is you're not ripping them off. You are really working, really answering calls. But...*(A beat)* I could never be part of this.

JIMMIE ALICE: *(Disappointed)* Ohhhh.

DAUBNEY: Why not?

VIJAY: Because I love India. For all I know, this plan could take work from relatives of mine. Do you know what families live on in India? Over a billion people and the average annual income per capita is the U S equivalent of under a thousand dollars. They need all the jobs they can get.

JIMMIE ALICE: *(Murmuring)* A billion people. Like China.

MELBA: Wait. Did you say under a thousand dollars? A month?

VIJAY: A year.

MELBA: Oh my god. How do they do that?

VIJAY: How do you think they do it?

DAUBNEY: Excuse me. Not to sound inhumane or
insensitive, but why the hell should I care? I mean,
I'm an American. They took away my job. They're
taking jobs away from my neighbors and friends.
I gotta look out for me and my wife. Come on.
America first. America's interests first.

VIJAY: I'm as American as you are, but that doesn't
mean I don't know or care about what's happening
to the rest of the world. When you're part of the world's
largest superpower, you should care even more about
the rest of the planet. It's your responsibility.

DAUBNEY: No. No, dude. Protectionism. We gotta
protect American workers.

VIJAY: Too much protectionism promotes isolationism.
You can't say "Capitalism is the American way", and
then penalize people from India, Mexico, Russia and
China when their companies embrace the free market,
compete with us as a result of globalization, and
are willing to do quality work for lesser salaries.
It's hypocritical.

DAUBNEY: You only got one country, dude. Pick a lane.

VIJAY: That's either/or thinking. A logical fallacy,
by the way. It doesn't promote sophisticated solutions
to complex world problems. I think I'd better go.
(He starts to rise.)

JIMMIE ALICE: *(Distraught)* Daub. You are insultin' my
new friend. You should apologize. *(Turning)* Vijay,
I'm sorry he said that—

DAUBNEY: Look, Vijay. Sorry I got heated. I just—
I just want you to do this protest with us. You seem

really cool. I mean, I want revenge against our old company and we need your help. *(To* JIMMIE ALICE *and* MELBA*)* It's a civil protest act, and we need you, as a fellow American. *(To* MELBA *and* JIMMIE ALICE*)* Can't you see him pitchin' this to Hodson? She'd cream all over him.

(A beat)

VIJAY: What'd you just say?

DAUBNEY: *(Cautiously)* Uh... Uh...I said that I could see you pitchin' us to one of the Ameriblaze V Ps. She'd dig you. Brainiacs rock her boat.

VIJAY: Ameriblaze? Hodson?

JIMMIE ALICE: Selena Hodson.

DAUBNEY: Really hot.

MELBA: I hope you never said that to her in the workplace. Sexual harassment. That's probably why we got canned—

(DAUBNEY rolls his eyes.)

JIMMIE ALICE: Please, Vijay—

VIJAY: *(Shifts)* Okay. I'll do it.

MELBA: What? Really?

DAUBNEY: You will?

JIMMIE ALICE *(Cheering)* Rah! Rah! Sisboombah!

VIJAY: Listen, I'll take the meeting with this woman. But that's it. You're going to have to work out all the other details yourselves. And you'd better make it good.

MELBA: But, but, but...we don't know anything about India.

JIMMIE ALICE: That's why I was lookin' for an India expert online. You gotta help us!

DAUBNEY: Vijay, won't you think about givin' us some Hindo lessons? I mean, don't you know Hindo?

JIMMIE ALICE: It's Hindi, Daub. Hindi. Even I know that much.

DAUBNEY: Whatever.

JIMMIE ALICE: You're so politically incorrect!

DAUBNEY: Sorry! I'm just a normal American. I watch Fox News. Does that flip you out, too, Jimmie?

JIMMIE ALICE: That's your problem—

MELBA: *(Pointedly)* Now, "kids..."

(VIJAY shakes his head, then continues.)

VIJAY: Look, I'm agreeing to this part of it...but after that, I'm out. I'm not going to support the exploitation of the culture and people of India. You're going to have to get your own asses in gear for the rest of the plan.

MELBA: But...but—we're not exploitin' them, are we?—

DAUBNEY: How do we know we can really even trust you?

VIJAY: You found me in the Arkansas Underground room. I wanted some action. So did you. Let's get the bastards at Ameriblaze! Your plan reminds me of those Sixties protests we've all studied in history class, sort of a wired twenty-first century version of a sit-in or something. So I'm down with it. When you think you're ready to execute, call me on my cell from a pay phone. A pay phone. Is someone going to keep track of what I'm about to say? It's procedural and pretty important. Jimmie Alice, can I trust you? You were my initial contact—

(JIMMIE ALICE nods, grabs a pencil and paper from her purse, and starting inscribing.)

VIJAY: Okay. Keep calling my cell until you reach me.
No messages. No e-mail. No faxes. No paper trails.
No voicemail. No texts. No I Ms. Nothing. When I hear
your plan, if my identity is not completely protected
and/or if I don't like it, I'll bail.

DAUBNEY: Just like that?

VIJAY: Just like that. So do your homework. I'll need
one week's lead time before the trip to Houston. And
of course, you're going to have to pay my way to
Houston, and for my hotel there, as well as expenses.
I'll be in disguise, so they won't be able to I D me.
And if this *ever, ever* comes out, or gets traced back
to me, I'll deny all of it. And, and, get—the A C L U
to help me press charges against you for—something.

(A moment of silence)

JIMMIE ALICE: Does this mean that you won't really be
in my political book group?

VIJAY: Yeah. Since it was bogus anyway, right? Al
Franken wrote *Lies and the Lying Liars Who Tell Them.*
That's the correct title. Any self-respecting book-loving
politico knows that.

*(VIJAY exits. JIMMIE ALICE looks forlornly at MELBA and
DAUBNEY.)*

DAUBNEY: Well, saw off my legs and call me Shorty.

JIMMIE ALICE: Well, hell's bells. What're we gonna do?

MELBA: I got some airline miles that I'll donate to get
him to Houston.

JIMMIE ALICE: Except that'll leave a paper trail back to
one of us...

MELBA: Damn. We need another plan.

DAUBNEY: Something invisible.

JIMMIE ALICE: How'll we learn some Hindi, and all about Indian culture?

DAUBNEY: Well, there's an Indian restaurant in Fort Smith. Quite a few more in Tulsa.

MELBA: That's so lame. Maybe we should just scrap it. Seriously. I gotta find a real job now, for my boys' sake. And we don't know if we can really trust this guy. *(She gets ready to leave.)*

JIMMIE ALICE: I need a job, too. And a new political book club member.

DAUBNEY: Now wait, wait. Don't bail.

MELBA: Get real, Daub. This was a good distraction to help us get over the shock. But we gotta move on. We can't live in denial. Protesting may be good for the soul, but it doesn't do a damn thing for the ole wallet.

DAUBNEY: Before we all give up, I know what we need. I know what's missin'.

JIMMIE ALICE: What?

DAUBNEY: Reece. Meet me tomorrow morning, ten sharp, at I-HOP.

(JIMMIE ALICE and MELBA react, as if they still have their doubts.)

MELBA: How're you gonna get him to show up? Are you gonna invite us all to breakfast?

JIMMIE ALICE: Pancakes on you, Daub? That's so nice. I like strawberries on mine—

DAUBNEY: No. Now, I bought y'all drinks just the other night. I'm gonna tell Reece we all need his help. Bad.

(Various reactions. Blackout)

Scene Five

(Lights up in a diner, the next morning. Seated in a booth, near center stage: DAUBNEY, JIMMIE ALICE, REECE *and* MELBA. *Everyone smiles at* REECE. *They all sip coffee.)*

DAUBNEY: So glad you could join us for coffee, Reece.

MELBA: Hey, Reece.

JIMMIE ALICE: I've missed ya.

REECE: Thanks. Missed ya, too, Jimmie A.

DAUBNEY: *(Looks at menu)* I could eat a quarter mile a' food. It all looks so larripin' good. *(Puts down menu.)* But I'd better not. How's the old job hunt comin', Reece?

REECE: Probably 'bout as good as yours. Now, cut to the chase. What do y'all want? I know you better than to think you'd just call me up to shoot the breeze in a diner on a Thursday morning.

*(*DAUBNEY, JIMMIE ALICE *and* MELBA *exchange glances.)*

DAUBNEY: Okay. We want to give you, as part of our old crew, another opportunity to be a part of a new company.

REECE: *(Suspiciously)* What new company?

DAUBNEY: This new company we're forming.

REECE: You're not still talking about that nutcase idea from the other night, are you? If so, I gotta go. *(Starts to stand up)* And by the way, has anyone bothered to contact Sam and Juanita with the bad news? Like maybe you, Daub? Since you were our Super?

(They all look at DAUBNEY.)*

DAUBNEY: No. But...but maybe we won't need to. Here's why I didn't. When they come back, they can work with us on this.

REECE: Daub, you're bonkers and chickenshit—

MELBA: Reece, hear us out, please. We got us a front man.

REECE: *(Stops)* Who? Who'd be so stupid?

JIMMIE ALICE: Well, actually, he's a brainiac. His name's Vijay Smith, and he's new in town—from New Jersey. He works as a freelance programmer.

MELBA: He's a real live radical politico.

JIMMIE ALICE: And a policy wonk.

DAUBNEY: But there's just one catch.

REECE: *(Sits back down)* There's always a catch with y'all. This'll be good.

DAUBNEY: He'll pitch us to Hodson, but we gotta learn all the Hindi stuff and set up everything else on our own.

MELBA: We've got to be able to sound Indian without his help.

DAUBNEY: And you already have the accent down.

REECE: *(Laughs)* Oh, oh, I see. Because I've seen *Monsoon Wedding* and *The Guru*, and a couple of Bollywood films, and y'all haven't, suddenly I'm the Hindi expert? Y'all're soooo cinematically deprived. Venture outta the multiplexes. Or go register at Netflix.

JIMMIE ALICE: I will, if I ever get another job.

DAUBNEY: Stay with me here. This guy Vijay's brilliant. He's agreed to sell us to Hodson. He's goin' there in disguise. He only wants airfare to Houston, and a few per diem expenses. All we have to do is train ourselves to "sound Indian". And the cash can start rollin' in again in a coupla weeks. And our revenge begins!

REECE: How's that? He's gonna take the jobs away from the company who took 'em away from us?

MELBA: *(Realizing)* I guess so. That means he'll have to really lowball our pitch against the people who took our jobs in India. Shit, that'll be a purty puny sum.

REECE: Right, so what sort of pittance are we talkin' about splittin' here? You can make up loony bin plans 'til the cows come home, but this makes no economic sense whatsoever.

DAUBNEY: *(Standing)* It's in the spirit of protest. Get it? It's us versus them. It's David versus Goliath. It's Paris, Arkansas, versus Houston, Texas. It's American blue collar workers versus all of India, Mexico, Russia and China. We're doin' it for the flag. But okay, okay. If patriotism is not enough... Listen, I'll kick in one month of my salary, to add to all of yours, just to get it rollin', as a show of faith.

REECE: *(Really suspicious)* That makes no sense, either. Why in hell would you do that?

MELBA: Yeah.

JIMMIE ALICE: Why?

DAUBNEY: Because...well, I made more money than y'all as Supervisor. And I feel real guilty that we got eighty-sixed. And 'cause I want to get back at Ameriblaze! Hey, haven't you ever been so pissed off that you'd do anything—*anything* to deliver royally F'ed up revenge to assholes who truly deserve it?

REECE: Not when the act of revenge is destructive to me. Lay off the Playstation, Daub.

MELBA: *(Pointedly)* Have you talked this over with Karen?

DAUBNEY: None of yer beeswax, missy.

JIMMIE ALICE: Personally, I prefer to leave revenge situations to karma.

DAUBNEY: A revenge plan's a hell of a lot quicker than karma. Here's what I want, more than anything: We land the Ameriblaze account. So the bastards get shafted! Big time.

MELBA: You know, Daub. You're kinda cute when you're mad.

REECE: *(To* DAUBNEY*)* You're a total Type A control freak.

DAUBNEY: And okay, okay. Reality time. This protest situation can't last long. I know it. You know it. Even if we land the account... But think of how much we would flat-out enjoy screwin' em back!

REECE: Paychecks feel good to me.

JIMMIE ALICE: Same here.

MELBA: Ditto.

DAUBNEY: To me, too. So in the meantime, we can be lookin' for new jobs. And if it turns out that takes a few months, at least we'll have some extra income on the side. Plus we can collect unemployment.

MELBA: Alleluia. At least that's somethin'. I don't want my boys to feel a pinch for long—

DAUBNEY: So add it up. You can live on that. And we can have corporate closure, knowing that we shafted the bastards back!

MELBA: Speaking of payment, exactly how *would* we get paid? Vijay said no trails.

(They all look at REECE.*)*

REECE: That part's not hard. He's a programmer, right? We'll dummy an account. The funds will be transferred online. He'll shadow-cache it. Any good hacker worth his salt can do it.

MELBA: But won't they need social security numbers? *(Snaps fingers)* No they won't. 'Cause we won't be U S citizens anymore, so no need for Ameriblaze to pay Social Security and all that other FICA stuff to the government either....

REECE: Righhhhhtt.

MELBA: So maybe they would just need dummy names and contact info.

DAUBNEY: Reece, you wanted proof that I didn't know we were gonna be axed. Well, here's your proof. If I'da known, would I risk my career, my entire future on this? The answer's no. So join our corporate protest *and* keep lookin' for a new job. If only our ancestors had the balls for an uprisin' then, this town might be thrivin' today—instead of just a backwater fishin' hole in the shadow of Mount Magazine. But we do have the balls. And we're havin' us a high-tech uprisin.' Join us!

JIMMIE ALICE: Come on. Please, Reece?

MELBA: It just ain't the same without ya.

(A beat)

REECE: Jimmie Alice, are you definitely doin' this?

JIMMIE ALICE: I am.

REECE: You can't be talked out of it?

JIMMIE ALICE: No, sir. I'm so burnin' furious. This is the most excitin' political protest I've ever heard of anywhere. I've waited my whole life for this.

(A beat)

REECE: Okay. This is completely against my better judgment, but I'm mad at those assholes, too. So yeah, while I'm lookin' for another job, I'll work on this little revenge project. But I'm doin' it for me. And I'm doin' it for the *innocent* Enron underlings, the ones who lost their jobs and pensions without any bailouts due to their greedy bosses. And all other low-on-the-ladder employees whose big fat corporate management left 'em out in the cold, hangin' by their butts, just for an almighty profit.

DAUBNEY: Cool, then—

REECE: But three conditions.

DAUBNEY: Oh, yeah? What?

REECE: One: As soon as I get another job, I'm outta here. Two: if anything goes wrong and it goes public, I'll blame you. 'Cause after all, it really is your idea. And Three: we're gonna do the culture immersion stuff my way. Deal?

(A beat)

DAUBNEY: *(Shrugs shoulders)* Deal.

MELBA: Deal.

JIMMIE ALICE: Show me the cards and deal, baby!

(They all put their hands in the middle of the table, crossing them, shaking to seal the deal. REECE does so reluctantly. Blackout)

Scene Six

(Lights up on split stage: JIMMIE ALICE *is at a pay phone, stage left. She dials. On the other side, a cell phone rings. Lights up on stage right, as* VIJAY *answers it.)*

JIMMIE ALICE: Yo, Vijay. It's me. Jimmie A. From the other day. Code word: Book group.

VIJAY: Hey.

JIMMIE ALICE: We got the money for your ticket. The safest thing's for you to book it yourself. Where do we hand it off?

VIJAY: I'll leave an address in your mailbox tonight. Tomorrow, put the money in a plain envelope and leave it in the mail slot of that address. But you must never, ever come there to find me—

JIMMIE ALICE: Got it.

VIJAY: Promise. You could be killed if you do. I mean it.

JIMMIE ALICE: *(Pausing)* Okay. I promise. And you'll set up the dummy account, cover it, and relay the data to us?

VIJAY: Yeah. It'll be fluid, but I think I can code it. No prob. So, I'll leave in a week. You prepped for the phone call?

(A beat)

JIMMIE ALICE: Yep.

VIJAY: You sure?

JIMMIE ALICE: We're almost ready. We're working it out. I want to make you so proud, Vijay. You got a good disguise? They'll have video monitors at Ameriblaze H Q.

VIJAY: Yeah, I've got a disguise. So I'll get in touch with Hodson. Let's synchronize our P D As. Eight days from now, around ten twenty-five A M. I'll call, as we discussed. Be ready to switch to a speakerphone with the group response.

JIMMIE ALICE: *(Takes note)* You got it. And thanks. *(A quick beat)* Will we ever see you around again?

VIJAY: Ya never know. See ya.

(VIJAY hangs up. Lights out on him.)

JIMMIE ALICE: Really, Vijay? Vijay?

(Blackout)

Scene Seven

(Lights fade up, back in JIMMIE ALICE's *living room, stage right. Various props, like clothes, charts, poker chips, etc. have been assembled.* JIMMIE ALICE, REECE, DAUBNEY *and* MELBA *seated in a half-circle, a little like a grade school "Show and Tell" presentation. There are pads of paper and pens scattered about.* REECE *looks at a list.)*

REECE: Okay. The first presentation's from Jimmie A.

JIMMIE ALICE: My information comes from "The People of India" web site, at: indiapunjabilt.com/ peopleofindia.htm.

DAUBNEY: Just get on with it.

MELBA: Take notes, Daub. And don't be such a crab.

(MELBA hands him a note pad and pen. Everyone takes notes at various points in the scene. JIMMIE ALICE *reads from a report, looking up as much as possible.)*

JIMMIE ALICE: According to this web site, some women wear traditional saris. A sari is a draped scarf worn like a skirt. There's regional variation in how you tie the scarf.

(JIMMIE ALICE *takes a beautiful cloth out of her purse and demonstrates tying it).*

DAUBNEY: Why in hell do I have to know how to tie a frickin' sari? You think someone is gonna ask "What are you wearing right now at 'Ameriblaze in Bangalore'?" We're not a sex line.

REECE: You said you'd do the cultural immersion my way. My way or the—

MELBA: Isn't that purty? And it covers your whole body. I'd eat at Dairy Queen every day if I got to wear a sari.

REECE: Doesn't Jimmie A. look great?

DAUBNEY: Can we go on? I didn't come here for a lil' fashion show—

JIMMIE ALICE: Jeez. You need to walk a mile in a sari, Daub. Walk some of this talk. Or how else will you sound believable to Hodson?

MELBA: Plus, hypothetically, we do have a dress code in our fake office in Bangalore. What if someone asks you about it?

DAUBNEY: *(Rolling his eyes)* It's a stretch but okay, okay.

JIMMIE ALICE: Now, guys. Some village and urban men wear a full-length cloth called a *dhoti*. In the north, they wear it tied with one or both ends brought between the legs, and tucked in, to form loose pant legs. *(She demonstrates this.)* In Punjab, many Sikh women wear a baggy pants and shirt outfit, the *salwar-kameez*. Men in northern India may also wear pants, the pajama-*kurta*.

MELBA: Did you say pajamas?

DAUBNEY: Next she'll say that Indians invented pajamas.

JIMMIE ALICE: Indians *did* invent pajamas. And guys, some men still wear the Nehru jacket.

DAUBNEY: Do they wear Nehru jackets with pajamas?

MELBA: The Beatles were into Nehru jackets...

DAUBNEY: Now you're datin' yourself.

MELBA: Well, that's better than datin' you.

DAUBNEY: Ha. I know you want me.

JIMMIE ALICE: Stop with the wisecracks, Daub. F Y I, it was named after India's first prime minister, Jawaharlal Nehru, who, with Gandhi, promoted non-violent liberation from British colonialism.

REECE: Excellent.

JIMMIE ALICE: It's all on the web site. Oh, and Muslims often wear different variations in clothin' than these. Otherwise, Western style clothin's increasingly worn.

DAUBNEY: Wait, wait. What was that about Muslims?

JIMMIE ALICE: There's a huge Muslim population in India. Duh.

DAUBNEY: No shit? Could Al-Qaeda be there? I wonder if our government's aware of this.

JIMMIE ALICE: Of course the government's aware of this, Daub. There're more Muslims in India than Buddhists and Christians. And just because they're Muslim doesn't mean they have a thing to do with Al-Qaeda, by the way. Sheesh. Can you be more politically incorrect? Or maybe you're just ignorant of all international issues 'cause you watch Fox News...

DAUBNEY: (*Sing-song*) Shut up, Jimmie A...

REECE: (*Looks at scarf*) Fascinatin'.

DAUBNEY: What?

REECE: Don't you find this stuff fascinatin'?

DAUBNEY: Yeah. About as fascinatin' as watchin' paint dry.

REECE: You go next, Daub, since you're in everyone's face already.

DAUBNEY: Fine. Currency—the rupee. That's R-U-P-E-E. One U S dollar equals so and so rupees, whatever the exchange rate is that day. *(From a plastic bag, he pulls out thirty-forty colorful poker chips or similar plastic circles. He puts them on the table and then holds up a dollar bill.)* This *(Indicates chips)* equals this. *(Indicates dollar)* Is that clear? Can I go on?

(Everyone nods.)

DAUBNEY: My next assignment was geography. Okay, the name of the capitol city, Bombay, was changed to "Mumbai" sometime in the nineties.

(Quick beat)

JIMMIE ALICE: Why?

DAUBNEY: *(Sighs)* I knew you're gonna ask that. This may be wrong, but I didn't get any of it from Fox News.com, Jimmie A. It's somethin' like this. Way back when, the Indians worshipped some god at a local temple by the name of Mumbadevi, and that was the city's original namesake. Then the Arabs came. Then the Portugese took the city from them in the fifteen hundreds. The Portugese renamed it the "Good Bay," but the British couldn't really understand 'em, and just heard something about "bays". Whatever, the British translated it wrong. So to remove the stamp of British colonialism, it's been changed back to something like the original name, Mumbai. But lots of Westerners and Indians still call it Bombay, 'cause ole colonial habits die hard or whatever. I bet some Indians would still say "Bombay" to Westerners on the phone. Who really knows? I do know this: Hodson won't know the F-in' difference. Okay, I'm done. *(He sits down.)*

(Everyone looks at each other. A beat)

MELBA: That's it on geography?

REECE: The whole country of India, one point two million beautiful square miles, and that's all you're gonna say 'bout the land?

DAUBNEY: Why the hell do we need to know any more 'bout geography?

REECE: Let's say someone asks where Bangalore is. Or what it's like. What'll we say? You didn't even tell or show us where Mumbai is.

DAUBNEY: Jeez. Are you gonna grade me, too? *(He sighs.)* Anybody got a map of India?

JIMMIE ALICE: Here. *(Holds it up)*

DAUBNEY: Would you point to Bombay?

(JIMMIE ALICE does, pointing to a west coast city, just below the center.)

DAUBNEY: You pass. Everyone happy now?

MELBA: So where's Bangalore?

(DAUBNEY looks at JIMMIE ALICE.)

REECE: No. You do it, Daub.

DAUBNEY: I have no idea, okay? I hope y'all are getting' off on humiliatin' your former Super.

MELBA: Yeah. We are. Big time.

JIMMIE ALICE: Bangalore's here.

(JIMMIE ALICE points to a southeastern/center region on the map. They all study it.)

DAUBNEY: Great. You want any more info, go to mapsofindia.com. Next?

MELBA: *(Stands up)* Me. Okay. Gear switch. Hang on to your hats. *(Clears throat)* My topic is home life. It's way too difficult to summarize India's social stuff in five minutes. So I'm just pullin' out some highlights that might come up on the phone. One: They got a ton of kids over there—somethin' around three or four hundred million *(She pulls out a construction cut-out of several kids in traditional dress holding hands)*. So, imagine millions of little tykes just like these, except three dimensional. Two: They still have some arranged marriages, and the wife marries into a family as an "outsider" in the Hindu tradition. Anyone else around here treat a wife like an outsider?

(MELBA looks pointedly at DAUBNEY. He shrugs.)

DAUBNEY: This is presentation, Mel, not an editorial.

MELBA: Fine. Three: The remnants of the caste system are still in effect.

JIMMIE ALICE: Just like here.

MELBA: We don't have a caste system.

REECE: Oh, really.

MELBA: We do?

(REECE gives her a long look.)

REECE: Wake up call, Mel.

JIMMIE ALICE: We've got major problems related to race, gender and class.

REECE: Surely you don't think we're all equal here.

MELBA: I know what the Constitution says.

REECE: *(Scoffing)* The Constitution—

DAUBNEY: Folks, folks, save it for the sociology blogs. Jeepers. You done, Mel?

MELBA: No. This info's from the Tulane University Children of India web site. *(She sits down.)* Now I'm done.

DAUBNEY: Aren't we getting' fancy. College web site. Can we finally get on to the most important stuff? Reece?

(REECE stands up and clears his throat.)

REECE: I've thought about the next topic, and knowing y'all as I do *(Clears his throat)*, I think you should go rent *Bend It Like Beckham.* The accents're British, and you'll understand a little more about Indian culture after you see it, even though it's set in England, and they're orthodox Sikhs. We're supposed to sound like we're speakin' British English. So it's good enough.

DAUBNEY: *Bend it Like Beckham.* Sounds like porn. Any bodacious babes in it?

MELBA: Just ignore him, everybody.

JIMMIE ALICE: It's a women's sports empowerment film, Daub.

DAUBNEY: Great. Another boring femi-Nazi chick flick...*(He scribbles.)*

REECE: Okay. I've prepared a small diagram with some differences between American English and Indian/ British English. *(Unrolls a large chart with the information listed below. He reads from it as he points.)* According to the *Cambridge University Encyclopedia for the English Language*, part of which I found online at a University of Michigan language web site. *(To DAUBNEY)* You should write this down. The biggest differences between the way we talk here in Arkansas and the way they talk English in India are: syllable stresses, some B/V confusion, the stops under the "T" and "D" sounds, different preposition idioms, word order, and puttin' "ing" on the end of things. Ameriblaze is likely givin' their new workers a chart that's the reverse of this.

(A beat. They look lost.)

DAUBNEY: Hell, Reece. Can't ya just give it to us in plain English?

REECE: *(Sighs)* 'Kay. Repeat after me. Ready?

(Their responses are varied in terms of how well they do the accent:)

REECE: "Amerivalaze."

MELBA, JIMMIE ALICE & DAUBNEY: "Amerivalaze."

REECE: "Can I be helping you, sir?"

MELBA, JIMMIE ALICE & DAUBNEY: "Can I be helping you, sir?"

(Blackout)

Scene Eight

(Lights up stage left, and these are bright lights in the glitzy big city Houston high-rise office of beautiful SELENA HODSON, one of the Ameriblaze V Ps. She sits behind a desk in a glamorous suit. VIJAY, now in a suit as well, sits opposite her. He is not disguised. A prepared tray with coffee cups and a pot is behind her.)

SELENA: Mister Smith. I'm Selena Hodson. Nice to meet you.

VIJAY: Ms Hodson. So great to meet you. Thanks for seeing me. Please call me Vijay.

(VIJAY hands SELENA a business card. She takes it. She motions for him to be seated.)

SELENA: Oh, it's Selena. We're not formal around here. We're already completely set in our staffing. But your phone pitch was so intriguing... So tell me more about... *(She looks at the card)* "The Beckham Group of Bangalore."

VIJAY: Well, I have a little start-up, a great call center crew there. If you need the best customer support, for the cheapest price, I've got the staff. Using the old family ties back home.

SELENA: Well, the timing isn't that great for Ameriblaze, because we just closed our office near Paris, Arkansas, and transferred the business to another company in Bangalore.

VIJAY: Who?

SELENA: Info-Indiaspeak. You know them?

VIJAY: Sure. That was set up by Jeremy Matta. They're good. There're lots of good companies available now, with the tax incentives that India gives to U S companies. Geography is history. But most of them have an annual forty percent turnover rate. We're better than any of them, and we keep our people longer. What kind of contract do you have with Info-Indiaspeak, if you don't mind me asking? Anything long term?

SELENA: *(Close to the vest)* No. It's limited.

VIJAY: Uh, huh. Well, that's good, because let me guess... You've gotten some customer complaints about Info-Indiaspeak already, haven't you?

SELENA: Maybe a few. How'd you know?

VIJAY: Because of the political climate we're in. You're seen as un-American if you outsource. Right? Your American customers want to vent about it. But the customers don't know that your boss loves the low numbers, and isn't going to go back to using expensive

American workers no matter what.... As *Forbes*
magazine says, the C E Os who use outsourcing all
get huge pay raises—

SELENA: Right. Well, we're a small company. We have
close ties with our product owners. Our customers
can tell that Info-Indiaspeaks's not in America.
They complain that the workers and customers can't
understand each other.

VIJAY: You need a better company in Bangalore, Selena.
Cut them loose and use us.

SELENA: *(Laughing, flirty)* Oh, now. I'm just gathering
info at this point. We'd have to pay out of the contract—

VIJAY: Believe me. We're so affordable. You'd still save
money doing that.

SELENA: *(Wide-eyed)* Really? Now you do have my
attention.

VIJAY: You know, if you're gonna outsource, you
should do it right, and feel good about it. It has a long
tradition. Most Americans don't even know its history.

SELENA: Well, I do know that most of our competitors
started outsourcing after 9/11, when the economy
tanked and the recession really hit rock bottom—

VIJAY: Outsourcing's not new. It's been around forever,
and it's not anti-American per se. It began with the
Industrial Revolution, when they first replaced workers
with machines. In fact, cloth makers in India in the
nineteenth century were among the first "victims"
of outsourcing, as cloth manufacturing became a
big British industry. It was the start of a new era:
Automation and the advent of the machine over
modern humans.

SELENA: Huh. *(She quickly moves the tray to the front of
her desk.)* Coffee? Black? Sugar? Milk?

VIJAY: Thanks. Black, please.

(SELENA *pours him a cup, then stands to bring it to him.
He takes it.*)

VIJAY: Let me tell you a little story, a true one. Time,
1811. Place, England. There's a band of weavers.
They're really good—top of their craft. They're so
talented they only have to work four days a week;
they can make their own hours since they're held in
such high regard by the market and the community.
But suddenly, boom. They hear that they, too, are
going to be completely replaced by big automated
steam machines. The machines were catching on,
but these worker-artists never thought that textile
industry would dare replace them.

SELENA: They got too comfortable, huh?

VIJAY: They were on top. They did beautiful fabric
handiwork—the best in the country. But replaced they
were. So the weavers got really angry. They started
talking about Robin Hood. They made up a fictional
mascot named Ned Ludd. Then, they protested. They
broke into the textile factories and smashed up all of the
weaving machines, completely destroying everything.

SELENA: I guess they really were pissed.

VIJAY: Yeah. I guess they were. So, the government
hears about this, and sends fourteen thousand British
soldiers to silence them. And that's the true story of
the Luddites.

SELENA: So the government stopped the backlash?

VIJAY: That's right, with thousands of troops. So you
see, historically, outsourcing has always been a
technological issue which intersects the socio-political.
And today, what do we remember of the Luddites?
Nothing about their magnificent protest. Nothing about
their attempt to save the local economy, artisans, and

a time-honored aesthetic. Oh, no. Today, we only think
of them as idiots who rejected technology, and we use
the term as a pejorative, for people who can't get on the
'Net, or people who won't text, or folks without iPods,
blackberries, blueberries, whatever. And that's how
all people who fight any new form of outsourcing will
be seen in the end—as Luddites who'll be left behind.
Anything that works cheaper and faster in business
will always be "better." You gotta embrace it.

SELENA: *(Impressed)* Wow. Thanks, Vijay. Now I feel a
lot less guilty for giving away so many American jobs.

*(SELENA gets up, takes his cup and pours more coffee from
the tray. She hands it to him. He takes it and slyly looks at
this watch as he does so.)*

VIJAY: (Rises, points out the window) Look,
outsourcing has been with us for years now. Your
medical tests are often outsourced to a technician in
India. That résumé you take to the nearest national
chain copy service is being hammered out by someone
in China or Mexico or Russia. In America, Catholic
priests don't have time to fulfill all the requests for
prayers, so they outsource the prayers to priests in
India. When you take your taxes into one of the big
national tax franchises, the work's prepped by an
Indian accountant. Eighteen states in America use
Indian workers to answer the state Welfare lines.
Hell, even wars are outsourced these days.

SELENA: They are?

VIJAY: Sure. Well over two hundred thousand fighters
in Iraq were hired from private defense companies like
Halliburton and Blackwater. They fight right along side
the U S troops, like a shadow army. *(Switches tactic)*
Hey, listen. I've got a crazy idea. Let's call my company,
and I bet when you hear them, you're gonna be amazed
at how good they sound. And you're gonna want to

sign us. Shall we? Just for the heck of it? For your consideration?

SELENA: I do have a meeting coming up soon....

VIJAY: It won't take long. I promise.

SELENA: *(Smiling. She buzzes an intercom.)* Ben, when's my next appointment?

MALE VOICEOVER: Eleven.

SELENA: Thanks, Ben. *(Back to* VIJAY*)* Okay. Let's do it. What time is it there?

*(*SELENA *moves a phone bank closer to him.)*

VIJAY: Night time. Eleven and a half hour difference. But my crew's always on the ball. Like so many night crews in Bangalore....

*(*VIJAY *dials a long number.* SELENA *watches. This is a dummy number, which begins with a country code to India, which is then patched to go to Paris, Arkansas.*

(A phone rings. Lights come up, stage right, in JIMMIE ALICE'S *place in Paris.* JIMMIE ALICE, DAUBNEY, REECE *and* MELBA *are gathered around a speakerphone.* DAUBNEY *motions for* JIMMIE ALICE *to answer it. She presses a button. Note: The action in these two scenes plays back and forth from one playing area to the other, but it is continuous action for both.)*

JIMMIE ALICE: *(With Indian accent)* Thank you for calling Beckham Group. How might I be helping you?

VIJAY: Greetings, Beckham Group. It's Vijay Smith. *(Pointedly)* Your boss.

*(*DAUBNEY *motions for them to all respond together.)*

MELBA, JIMMIE ALICE, REECE *&* DAUBNEY: Hi, Vijay. Are you having a good day?

SELENA: *(To* VIJAY*)* They're good.

VIJAY: *(Nodding)* Yes. Thanks. I'm here with Ms Selena Hodson, a Vice President of Ameriblaze. I told her that you were smarter, faster, cheaper and better workers than anyone else. But I know that you'll sell yourselves far better than I can. Why don't you tell her a little about yourselves?

(DAUBNEY *motions "1, 2, 3" and then:)*

MELBA, JIMMIE ALICE, REECE & DAUBNEY: Amerivalaze, how can we be helping you, madame?

SELENA: I'd like to meet you one at a time, please. *(She takes notes as they speak.)* Let me hear from one of the women, first, please.

(DAUBNEY *pushes* MELBA *to the speakerphone.)*

MELBA: *(With some Indian accent)* Hello, Madame Vice President Hodson. I'm Madhu. My name means honey. I am thirty, and mother of one. My family sends blessings and hopes you will hire us.

(MELBA *makes an obscene gesture to the phone.* DAUBNEY *points to* REECE.)

REECE: *(With some Indian accent)* Hello, Madame Vice President Hodson. I'm Ransik. I'm twenty-three. Is it hot and muggy in Houston today?

SELENA: Why, yes, Ransik. How did you know?

(VIJAY *alternates between grimacing and acting like everything's all right as the Arkansas crew speaks.)*

REECE: The Weather Channel International.

(DAUBNEY *pushes* JIMMIE ALICE *to the speakerphone.)*

SELENA: I see—

JIMMIE ALICE: Hey. I'm Jeevan. My name means life. Long life to you. Do you eat yogurt and take yoga in Houston? Namaste.

SELENA: Why, yes, I do, Jeevan. Thanks. I'm only Level Two in Power Yoga. Namaste to you.

DAUBNEY: And last, I'm Darpan. That means mirror. I love the N B A. Do you follow the N B A?

SELENA: No, sadly I never have the time—

DAUBNEY: The N B A basketball star Yao Ming. Another example of good outsourcing. Bye.

SELENA: *(To* VIJAY, *she laughs)* Okay. That was great. But let's see how they do on idioms. Beckham Group, one by one. If I say I'm "rolling in dough", what does it mean? Um, Madhu, I believe it was, your question—

*(*DAUBNEY *pushes* MELBA *up to the speakerphone.)*

MELBA: Rolling in dough means you are rich, madame. You could also say you are loaded.

SELENA: *(Nodding with approval)* Hm. Excellent. Next was Ransik, I believe. If I tell you not to put all your eggs in one basket, it means what?

*(*REECE *steps up again.)*

REECE: It means to diversify your portfolio.

SELENA: *(To* VIJAY) They are unbelievable. How did you train them? Just a couple more. *(She refers to her notes.)*

*(*VIJAY *nods.)*

SELENA: Jeevan, if you are dodging a bullet, what are you doing?

JIMMIE ALICE: Um, you are nicely avoiding a big problem.

SELENA: Yes! I just can't stump them. Finally, Darpan, if I'm looking for a needle in a haystack, what am I doing?

DAUBNEY: You are wastin' your time.

SELENA: Right again. Excellent.

VIJAY: Okay. Thanks, Beckham Group—

SELENA: Wait. Wait. Can I ask them one more thing?

VIJAY: *(Warily)* Sure. What?

SELENA: *(Back to speakerphone)* If you're talking to
Americans, you have to be ready for anything,
Beckham Group. So I always give any crew an off-the-
wall test—uh oh, that's idiomatic, too, but you probably
know what it means—something that would never
really happen, but which shows how fast you think
on your feet, and how creative you can get in a
situation that takes you off the prepared script.
It's very challenging to talk with angry Americans,
especially about their software problems. Okay?
So here's my final test for you. This will reveal more
about your true natures. *(She thinks for a second.)*
Sing me one of your favorite local songs. Something
with a true Bangalore beat.

*(In Arkansas, total panic sets in. They motion to each other:
"What do we do?")*

VIJAY: *(Alarmed)* Oh, there's not a musician among
them, Selena. I can assure you. You don't want to
hear something like that. Isn't there another test—

SELENA: Oh, yes. Yes I do want to hear them. It would
do my soul good. Please. I love world beat. Anything
from India! One of your childhood favorites would be
fine! Just a local song—

VIJAY: No, really, you don't want to hear—

SELENA: Yes, really, I do.

VIJAY: They are so shy-and tone deaf—

SELENA: They can't be shy and tone-deaf, they're phone
workers. They have to listen and talk to strangers all
day long. They've got to detect nuance, calm people

down, and handle almost anything, improvise and placate—

VIJAY: But they don't speak daily to important Vice Presidents in Houston and they don't sing to anyone but their kids, and this test probably makes them very nervous, and they won't be at their best—

SELENA: Do you want this account or not? It's definitely making you nervous, Vijay. You're starting to sweat—

(SELENA *hands* VIJAY *a tissue. He takes it and blots his face.*)

(*During this last exchange,* DAUBNEY *motions to everyone to step up to the speakerphone. No one will.* MELBA *motions for* DAUBNEY *to start. She mouths "You" to him. Various other things like this go on, with everyone motioning "You", "No" or "No way".*)

(*Then* DAUBNEY *just starts pounding rhythmically on the table or floor, to a "1, 1, 2" rhythm. After a few more seconds of this,* JIMMIE ALICE *valiantly steps up to the speakerphone and sings, in an Indian sounding melody and modality, reading off of her "Show and Tell" index card:*)

JIMMIE ALICE: Kameeeeeeez, kameeeeeeez, sari, sari. Nehruuuuuuuu, Nehruuuuuuuu, dhokti, dhokti."

(*More chaos in Paris, more frantic motions... Then* MELBA *steps up, and moves her hands in snake-dancing motions. She also reads from her notes. She takes off one of her earrings and starts shaking it towards the speakerphone.*)

MELBA: The families of India, ayeeeeee, ayeeeee. Bless the families of India, ayeeeeee, ayeeee."

(MELBA *steps away, shrugs and points to* DAUBNEY. REECE *motions "No way."* DAUBNEY *indicates that someone else has to take over the drumming.* JIMMIE ALICE *and* MELBA *start drumming.* VIJAY, *in front of* SELENA, *has to mask his reaction to the performance.*)

DAUBNEY: Rupee, rupeeeeeeee, rupee, rupee.
Not Bombay, yes Bombay, and Mumbai, Raji."

*(JIMMIE ALICE and MELBA look at REECE with desperation
in their eyes. REECE begrudgingly goes to the speakerphone,
and with his verse, the melody changes to different modality,
a major chord sound:)*

REECE: Shiva, Kali, hear our songs. *(He stands.)* Krishna,
Arjuna, right our wrongs."

*(DAUBNEY executes a brief percussion solo. REECE motions
for everyone to go back to MELBA's verse for the ending.
Then REECE, JIMMIE ALICE, DAUBNEY and MELBA finish
big together, and the initial modality.)*

MELBA, JIMMIE ALICE, REECE, & DAUBNEY:
The families of India, ayeeeeee.
Bless the families of India, ayeeeeee."

(They stop. Moment of silence)

(Then SELENA applauds.)

SELENA: *(To speakerphone)* That was wonderful!
Wonderful. *(To VIJAY)* So heartfelt! What did it
all mean?

VIJAY: It's a complete utter nonsense. Meaningless.

SELENA: Like a nursery rhyme?

VIJAY: *(Shaking his head)* Not even.

SELENA: *(Back to speaker phone)* Beckham Group, anyone
who can be that good on the spur of the moment with
such an off-the-wall request would do wonderfully
well with prepared scripts. Great stuff! Your boss and
I are going to work out some terms. Congratulations.
You've got the job. And welcome to Ameriblaze.

(She shakes VIJAY's hand. Lights out on them.)

DAUBNEY: She swallowed it hook, line and sinker!

(JIMMIE ALICE *and* MELBA *cheer. The foursome exchange
high fives in* JIMMIE ALICE's *living room, although* REECE
seems wary, and less exuberant than the others. Crossfade to:)

Scene Nine

(Near center stage, VIJAY *and* SELENA *are seated in a
candlelit restaurant. They each have wine glasses.* SELENA's
*suit jacket is off. They both have contracts out, visible to the
side of their place settings. There's an opened bottle of wine
on the table. They have finished eating dinner.)*

SELENA: Looks like we're down to the fine print.
Congratulations.

VIJAY: Yes, that about wraps it up. Congrats to you, too.

(They clink glasses.)

SELENA: This deal went faster than most.

VIJAY: Have you done a lot of these overseas
negotiations?

SELENA: *(Cautiously)* A few.

VIJAY: You know, it's funny. Our wired culture has
made it possible for the world to participate in this
romanticized dream—America's meritocracy—but
without actually setting foot on these shores. And at
first, many of the workers doing the outsourced jobs
feel like they are, in a small way, part of America.
They talk to Americans, they have to think like
Americans. They think about American food, American
politics, American music, American fashion, American
life. They have to try to understand Americans, if only
for ten minutes at a time.

SELENA: They get to fight with Americans.

VIJAY: They feel just a little tiny bit American.

SELENA: That's good. That works for us. It makes them try to relate to the customers more.

VIJAY: And the irony is that after awhile, some of them get really sick of Americans. They come to pity Americans, maybe even hate Americans.

SELENA: I think anybody working a call center job gets sick of the customers, period.

VIJAY: "Familiarity breeds contempt."

SELENA: "All that glitters is not gold."

VIJAY: *(Smiling)* I'm surprised that you were able to make this deal without visiting our facility.

SELENA: I was just in Bangalore. I don't need to go right back.

VIJAY: When were you there?

SELENA: A month ago. We've just moved...a lot of business there.

VIJAY: That doesn't sound good.

SELENA: Oh, it's fine.

VIJAY: What happens when you're done with the Indian workers, when they get too expensive for Ameriblaze?

SELENA: We already have plans for China. *(Shift)* Let's not talk about work anymore.

VIJAY: Okay.

SELENA: So....What else do you like to do?

VIJAY: What do you mean?

SELENA: You know, like, for fun.

VIJAY: Well, let's see. You mean when I'm not traveling?

SELENA: Right. As in let's say, you're at home. In your boxers. Or whatever. What would you be doing right about now?

(A quick beat)

VIJAY: I like to read.

SELENA: So do I. In bed?

VIJAY: In bed. Or wherever. I like to read just about anywhere.

SELENA: That's amazing. Me, too. You married?

VIJAY: No. You?

SELENA: No.

(VIJAY reaches for the wine bottle and pours them both more wine. They each take a drink.)

VIJAY: Divorced?

SELENA: Yeah. It's been five years. But I'm still good friends with my ex. I still give him...a lot of support. You ever been married?

VIJAY: No.

SELENA: It works with the right person. But you've both got to be at the same speed. You know what I mean?

VIJAY: Yeah. I know exactly what you mean.

SELENA: You got a girl back in Bangalore?

VIJAY: Not yet.

SELENA: Good.

VIJAY: Why?

SELENA: Because I'd like to really seal this deal. You know what I mean?

(VIJAY reacts. Blackout)

Scene Ten

(Next evening. Lights come up on JIMMIE ALICE's *house. Lighting: there are some shadows.* JIMMIE ALICE *wears a sari, and a headset.* MELBA, *wearing a headset, sits in a lotus position.* REECE, *also wearing a headset, spoons yogurt out of container.* DAUBNEY, *wearing a turban on his head, stands at the window, looking out, his back to audience.* DAUBNEY *wears a headset, too. As each Arkansas crew worker gets a call, a small light on a phone bank lights up.)*

DAUBNEY: Gettin' cloudy out there. Hope it won't mess with our satellite bounce.

JIMMIE ALICE: *(Into headset)* Amerivalaze. How may I be helping you, sir or madame or child?

MELBA: *(To* DAUBNEY*)* You know, the calls don't really seem to be comin' that fast.

DAUBNEY: Well *(He turns)*, that li'l Indian company probably lost a lot a' people for us 'cause no one could make hide nor hair of what they were sayin'.

MELBA: In two weeks? That's awful fast to lose such a big cut of the customer base—

REECE: Amerivalaze. Can I be helping you, madame or miss?

DAUBNEY: *(To caller:)* Amerivalaze. May I be of assistance?

REECE: You may register at our web site. And we thank you many times for calling us with Amerivalaze. *(To* MELBA*)* Hey, Melba. You're right. There's some sort of delay. It's probably due to all the dummy number transfers and call forwards...I'll check out how long the delays are... *(He starts timing lapses on his watch.)*

MELBA: 'Kay. *(She gets a call.)* Amerivalaze. I thank you for your phone call and send many blessings to your home. What is it that I may be doing for you today?

JIMMIE ALICE: And we thank you with devout joy for calling this Amerivalaze help center.

DAUBNEY: Many thanks for calling Amerivalaze. Namaste.

MELBA: And we thank you for calling Amerivalaze. We wish you health and long life.

REECE: Whoa. We've got thirty seconds between calls.

JIMMIE ALICE: Do we? Well, all I know is that I feel much less stress workin' this way than I ever did at the call center.

DAUBNEY: Yeah. That's because you're takin' half of the number of calls you got previously, and making a third of the pay. Plus you're workin' from home.

MELBA: I don't know how families in India make it on this little pay. I really don't.

REECE: Right now, it still sucks to be us.

JIMMIE ALICE: Yeah I know. But I feel better. You know what I mean?

MELBA: Yeah. There's more time to breathe.

JIMMIE ALICE: One thing I've been wonderin' 'bout is the Kashmir conflict.

DAUBNEY: What the hell?

JIMMIE ALICE: The Kashmir region—the beautiful section in the Himalayas that's long been disputed between India and Pakistan. It's produced a lot of bloodshed between 'em—two wars since 1947. You should read about it, you know, Daub. It's important world history.

DAUBNEY: You got something against American history?

MELBA: I've been worryin' about the nuclear build-up between Pakistan and India.

DAUBNEY: *(Shakes his head)* Why don't y'all relax and just worry yourselves about what's best for the ole U S of A?

REECE: *(Still looking at watch)* And we're over and out. Hey, gang. We're done. Shift over. It's the weekend. No overnights. *(He punches a bunch of numbers out on the phone bank.)*

MELBA: Hooray!!!

REECE: I'm outta here.

(JIMMIE ALICE starts to clear some of their dishes to the kitchen.)

REECE: Jimmie A, you need help with any of that?

JIMMIE ALICE: No, I'm cool.

REECE: 'Kay. 'Night, all.

MELBA, JIMMIE ALICE and DAUBNEY: 'Night.

(REECE exits stage left. JIMMIE ALICE clears dishes to the kitchen, off right. MELBA helps by taking other dishes into the kitchen. She exits. DAUBNEY is alone in the room now. He looks towards the kitchen. He quickly boots up JIMMIE ALICE's laptop, and starts punching numbers into the keyboard. MELBA re-enters again. DAUBNEY doesn't hear her. She watches him for a few seconds from behind, then:)

MELBA: Daub, what're you doin'?

(DAUBNEY is immediately startled, and stops. He turns off the computer and turns around.)

DAUBNEY: How long were you back there, Melba, sweetie?

MELBA: A coupla seconds. What's up?

(DAUBNEY *turns to her and takes off the turban.*)

DAUBNEY: Nothin'. Nothin'. Hey, Melba. You look really good tonight. Wanna go get a drink?

MELBA: Right now?

DAUBNEY: Yeah. You free?

MELBA: Uh, yeah...I have to make a quick call to one of my exes.

(DAUBNEY *crosses to* MELBA *and puts his arm around her waist. He then draws her closer to him.*)

DAUBNEY: Then make it.

MELBA: Hey. What's the scoop between you and Karen?

DAUBNEY: *(Sighing)* I was about to ask Jimmie A if I could spend the night on this here couch.

MELBA: I think we can find somethin' more comfortable for ya than that.

DAUBNEY: I think so, too.

(Blackout)

Scene Twelve

(A few hours later, in JIMMIE ALICE'*s house. She's alone, again with two and a half empty beer bottles on her table. She starts to tap on the keyboard on her laptop. But it doesn't respond to her commands. She taps again. She tries to override some commands. Frustrated, she picks up the phone and dials. Split stage: the stage lights up on the left;* REECE *answers the phone in a bathrobe.)*

REECE: Hello.

JIMMIE ALICE: Hey, Reece.

REECE: *(Surprised)* Jimmie Alice. Hey.

JIMMIE ALICE: Hey. You got a sec?

REECE: Hey, yeah. What's up? You all right?

JIMMIE ALICE: Yeah, yeah. Sorry for the bother. I just wanted to run somethin' by ya, if it's not too late.

REECE: Sure thing. Shoot.

JIMMIE ALICE: I don't know why, but I think someone's programmed a delay at this end on our calls. *(Dramatic pause)* Reece, we have us a saboteur.

REECE: A saboteur. Here? You sure?

JIMMIE ALICE: I swear. In our very midst.

REECE: It ain't me, babe.

JIMMIE ALICE: I know. That's why I'm tellin' ya.

REECE: How do you know it's not me?

JIMMIE ALICE: Because you left my place before this block was put on my computer, according to my internal log. I could override the block through my own wily ways.

REECE: Okay. Now, let's say it's someone really clever tryin' to trick us. Maybe you're the saboteuse, and you're tryin' to pull wool over my eyes by alertin' me to this—

JIMMIE ALICE: So how do you know it ain't me? I hear that. Well, all I can say is I was in the kitchen doin' dishes when this little virus time-bomb was planted on my software. You know what time you left. This happened 'bout four minutes later. I was doin' the dishes alone. You're gonna have to take me at my word.

(A pause)

REECE: 'Kay. I believe you.

JIMMIE ALICE: 'Kay. So that leaves Melba and Daubney.

REECE: I highly doubt it's Melba. She's no computer nerd. Logically, that leaves Daub...

JIMMIE ALICE: But why would Daub be tryin' to kill the system?

REECE: Dunno. But you did the right thing by callin' me, Jimmie A.

JIMMIE ALICE: That's 'cause I trust you. I know you're always lookin' out for me.

REECE: Am I? I guess so. Now get some shuteye. You 'n I'll tackle this again in the mornin'.

JIMMIE ALICE: 'Kay.

REECE: 'Night.

JIMMIE ALICE: 'Night.

(They both hang up, and sort of look at the phone after hanging up. Then blackout)

Scene Thirteen

(Lights up on SELENA, *back in Houston in her office. She dials a number, then, frustrated, presses the intercom button.)*

SELENA: *(Into intercom)* Ben? You sure you gave me the right number for Vijay Smith? You triple-checked it?

MALE VOICEOVER: Yes, Selena. Oh, F Y I. More complaints on the customer service responses. And... *(Ominously)* Murphy wants to see you right away. A S A P. Something's going down.

SELENA: *(Sarcastically)* Greeeeaaat.

MALE VOICEOVER: Have a nice life.

SELENA: Yeah, you have a nice life, too, Ben. *(She dials a number one more time, then hangs up in frustration.)* That bastard Vijay, if that was even really his name! Where the hell'd he go? And what'd he done to Ameriblaze?

(Blackout)

Scene Fourteen

(The next day. Lights come up on JIMMIE ALICE'S *living room, S R.* MELBA *enters and* JIMMIE ALICE *enter from the kitchen. They carry coffee cups. Note:* JIMMIE ALICE *wears a different outfit than in the previous scene.)*

JIMMIE ALICE: Shall we do some downward facin' dogs before the guys get here?

MELBA: *(Glowing)* Sure. I need a good stretch after the wild night I had.

(They put their coffee cups down on a table, and assume the yoga position. They go into a sun salute routine.)

JIMMIE ALICE: Oh, yeah? What kinda wild night was that? Did you go over to Clarksville or somethin'?

MELBA: Okay, Jimmie A. I'm gonna tell you what happened. But you can't tell a soul. No one. You hear me? You swear?

JIMMIE ALICE: I swear. Spill it, sister.

MELBA: Daub and me. *Finally.*

JIMMIE ALICE: Really? Has he left Karen?

MELBA: She kicked him out two days ago.

(They both stand up again.)

JIMMIE ALICE: Why?

MELBA: That part I didn't get to hear. And he didn't stay all night, either. I don't know where he went. He got a call on his cell and split at two A M, all upset—

(REECE enters from the front door.)

REECE: Mornin', y'all.

JIMMIE ALICE & MELBA: 'Mornin.

REECE: Time to "go live". Where's our fearless ex-leader?

JIMMIE ALICE: Haven't seen him.

(They put on their headsets. But JIMMIE ALICE *can't get her computer to boot. She looks at* REECE, *as if to say, "Here's what I was talking about last night.")*

JIMMIE ALICE: It's dead.

MELBA: Your computer's dead?

JIMMIE ALICE: Damn! Somebody's messed with it.

REECE: *(Looking at computer)* It's not just the computer. *(Picks up her phone)* Your landline's completely dead, too.

JIMMIE ALICE: This is freakin' me out—

MELBA: Weird! Who would messed with your phone line? I hope to heaven you haven't been hangin' out with some creepy anti-social serial killer type chat room guys again—

JIMMIE ALICE: No. I swear.

*(*DAUBNEY *comes in through a front entrance. He's breathless. He's a complete wreck, disheveled; he's slept in his clothes if he's slept at all...)*

DAUBNEY: There's two police cars headed this way. We gotta bail. Go everyone! Now! Now!

(Utter pandemonium in response)

MELBA: What do you mean "headed"?

JIMMIE ALICE: What do you mean "bail"?

REECE: What the hell is goin' down, Daub? Come clean.

DAUBNEY: I, uh, I saw these two patrol cars on the highway behind me, lights on top all awhirl. *(Looks around)* Are there any disks lyin' around? We gotta flush 'em fast. And where're the Indian scripts? We gotta flush those, too. *(He frantically tries to gather evidence. He picks up any papers that he sees.)*

JIMMIE ALICE: Won't all that wreck my septic tank?

MELBA: Which highway?

REECE: Now calm down, everyone. Daub, I mean it. Come clean or—

DAUBNEY: Look, okay. Okay. Look, I do know somethin'. I, uh...I better tell you while we have a chance. They've arrested Hodson in Houston.

MELBA: What?

JIMMIE ALICE: What for?

REECE: And how'd you find out?

DAUBNEY: Some little birdie told me. So if they got her, that means someone's comin' for us next. We gotta destroy all papers, disks, everything!

REECE: Why've you been in touch with someone who knows Hodson?

JIMMIE ALICE: Yeah. Explain that, mister.

MELBA: Yeah.

DAUBNEY: Jeez. Can't a guy get any support 'round here? We're 'bout to go down, gang—

REECE: You'd better tell us whatever you got right now. If cops really are comin', I'm so damn pissed that I'll tell 'em everything to nail you—

DAUBNEY: Okay. Okay. Okay. Hodson and me...we were havin' an affair. Long distance-like. Whenever we could. Whenever she was here. Whenever I was there.

MELBA: Ewwwwwww.

JIMMIE ALICE: And that's why you been havin'
problems with Karen.

DAUBNEY: Yeah. She caught on.

REECE: You were sleepin' your way to the top? Pathetic.
And at your age.

DAUBNEY: Do you want to hear the rest or not? I'm
almost outta here... *(Tries to take a pile of papers into the
kitchen.)*

REECE: No, you're not. *(He blocks the kitchen door.)*

DAUBNEY: Okay. So, she dumps me, see. Selena dumps
me outta the blue. Right after she was here a coupla
weeks ago. *(He pulls out a handkerchief made out of
material which resembles an American flag and dabs his face.)*

JIMMIE ALICE: And then we got outsourced—

MELBA: And that's why you were pissed—

DAUBNEY: Can you blame me? I was in love with her—

REECE: And so you got us all in on this elaborate
scheme just so you could get back at your ex-lover?

JIMMIE ALICE: Why you—

REECE: I never did trust ya, Daub, but I sure as hell
didn't know that you were this big an asshole and
as dumb as a post—

MELBA: You put us all in jeopardy because of your
wounded dick—and after what we did last night—
ewwwwwww, ewwwww, ewwwwww.

REECE: *(To* JIMMIE ALICE*)* What'd they do last night?

*(*JIMMIE ALICE *makes a motion with her hand)*

DAUBNEY: Fine. Fine. I'm not proud.

REECE: We gotta learn, folks. Never never trust an impulsive selfish nutcase leader who's passionate about a half-cocked plan that doesn't make any sense, and doesn't have an exit strategy. Especially if he's wavin' a flag.

DAUBNEY: Cry in your soup without me. I'm outta here.

(VIJAY *enters, dressed in a suit.*)

VIJAY: Not so fast.

DAUBNEY: *(Scoffing)* You? Has the Magical Mystery Tour come to take me away?

VIJAY: Vijay Smith, F B I. You're under arrest, Daubney Camp. You have the right to remain silent... *(He displays handcuffs.)*

DAUBNEY: What? F B I? *What??????*

REECE: *(Shaking his head)* He's too dumb to remain silent.

MELBA: Daub???

JIMMIE ALICE: Vijay?

VIJAY: Anything you say can and will be used against you. Let's go. *(Starts to take* DAUBNEY *offstage, motions as if to indicate to others to be ready ...)* Move it, Camp.

(VIJAY *and* DAUBNEY *exit.*)

DAUBNEY: *(As he exits.)* Noooooooooooooooooooo. I'm gonna write a book from prison. Someone, call C N N.

VIJAY: Come on, Camp.

DAUBNEY: *(Offstage)* This isn't finished yet. Not by a long shot. I'm gonna be a best-sellin' folk herooooooooooooo. *(His voice trails away offstage.)*

JIMMIE ALICE: That was Vijay!

REECE: Whoa. Whoa.

MELBA: My head's hurtin'. Is this a dream?

(VIJAY *re-enters.*)

VIJAY: Hi, again. Sorry about all this. *(To* REECE*)* I don't believe we've met. I'm Vijay Smith.

REECE: *(Extends hand)* Reece Howard. Nice to meet you.

VIJAY: Same here. I recognize your voice from our wire-tapping.

REECE: So're we under arrest, too, Mister Smith?

VIJAY: Call me Vijay. No, although you may be subpoena'd as witnesses later. Here's what we know so far. When Jimmie Alice posted in the Arkansas Underground chat room two weeks ago, she used terms that triggered the F B I surveillance squad. So I was sent to investigate you. We thought you were domestic terrorists and/or trying to link to Al-Qaeda.

JIMMIE ALICE: Oh my god.

MELBA: Oh my god. I'm gonna faint.

JIMMIE ALICE: I'm sorry, guys. I guess I'd had too much to drink—

VIJAY: So I came to check you out. After I met you, I figured out that there was something hinky going on, but that you weren't terrorists.

MELBA: Thank God.

VIJAY: When I went to Houston, I also found out some stuff on Ameriblaze and Hodson, whose name I recognized from an I R S alert. For example, they were outsourcing everything. Everything. Ameriblaze was going belly-up, but Hodson was trying to hide it by sending all departments to India in order to completely avoid paying all U S taxes. That's illegal. So with the I R S, we got Ameriblaze for tax evasion.

REECE: But what was Daubney tryin' to do with the computers here?

VIJAY: He wanted revenge, pure and simple. So he planted a virus to take down Ameriblaze's entire computer network. And that's a federal crime. He also programmed busy signals on most of your incoming calls.

REECE: I wondered how he knew the term "corporate malfeasance". Remember when he said "corporate malfeasance" at the bar that time? He probably heard it in pillow talk with Hodson.

MELBA: *(Collapsing in chair)* What a piece of work.

VIJAY: Hodson? *(He coughs. Pause)* Yeah. So you're in the clear because we tapped all your wires. We know that none of you knew about any of that other stuff. *(More quietly:)* And, just between us, I thought some of your political ideas were interesting. Sorry we didn't get a chance for further debate. *(Back to business:)* Anyway, F Y I, we've barricaded this street for a few hours, while the evidence squad takes away a few items. But it should be all clear in a couple of hours. The phones are back on. Have some coffee and relax. We'll stay in touch. And thanks. *(He exits through the front, then turns back around.)* Oh, I almost forgot. There's a couple outside who says they know you all. They're back from vacation. Sam and Juanita?

REECE: Yes, yes, we know 'em. We'll come say "Hi". Thanks.

(VIJAY waves and exits.)

JIMMIE ALICE: You know what I'm thinkin'. All this shock and misery, and we still don't have jobs.

REECE: I think we're gonna have to start all over again, ya know?

MELBA: How? I got two boys to raise, Reece. I need money now.

REECE: Well, I don't know exactly. But these jobs we had, they're gone. We gotta look around, and try and see where the world's headin' next, and see how we can work differently. Time's have changed. We may have to take certain jobs to get by, and plan ahead by startin' the new ones-the ones we can see the future with— in our spare time. But we gotta grow now, and keep the whole world in our sights.

JIMMIE ALICE: Reece, you oughta start a company. You'd be a great boss.

MELBA: Good idea!

REECE: Hey, ya know. Maybe I will. Or maybe you will. Or maybe we will together. *(A transition)* What d'ya say, let's go talk to Sam and Juanita...

MELBA: I nearly forgot they're waitin'.

(They turn to the front door, open it, and wave excitedly. REECE, MELBA and JIMMIE ALICE look out together.)

MELBA & JIMMIE ALICE: *(Staggered/almost in unison)* Hey, y'all. Welcome home! How are you doin'?

(JIMMIE ALICE and MELBA exit. Lights down on the rest of the stage; REECE is lit as he sits at the computers. He boots up the computer. He sees that it's working again already; he's pleased. He types as he talks:)

REECE: Here we go. "Wanted: Three people...no, five people looking for like-minded fired call center workers to start a business where people actually appreciate them, committed to keeping jobs in America. Details available soon. Interested parties, please e-mail us at this address or phone 479 555-9802. Operators are standing by...." No. "Americans are standing by."

(REECE freezes. Blackout)

END OF PLAY